The vault

Treasure

Q. BANKS

Table of Contents
The vault 3

The vault

The story starts with a splendid kid named Tom who, in his school days, tackles a tremendous issue like the Mexican oil slick, which makes the large oil organizations all over the planet popular before he completes school. Eight of the biggest oil organizations on the planet extended to him an employment opportunity and a compensation of 400,000 bucks each year, however the offers were high to the point that he needed to open a protected with the assistance of his sharp brain. Based on what was viewed as a difficult protected, this safe really contained something that Walter needed to accomplish, yet the past oneAfter 80 years nobody has had the option to open this puzzling vault Walter acquaints Tom with his group.

I concealed endless fortunes, however the Spence government before long learned about it and seized all that Walter found and secured it in the protected of a Spanish frenzy. Mila, who was skilled at changing any camouflage for her central goal, likewise had Klaus in her group, who was a splendid programmer, James Wall Simon, who brought everything required for her group as long as she got the cash, she gave Walter the world. could bring everything except today was Tom's most memorable day and the group was struggling with hacking the bank's framework they expected to fill in the code however they had no clue about what the code could be then Tom concedes that he got a computerized phone message from a bank client. At last Tom's stunt worked and he got the code without any problem. Everybody praised Tom and Tom showed up at his new home. Tom alongside the remainder of the group started to figure out the guide of the Bank of Spain. As per Walter, this building is the most hazardous structure on the planet since there are great many sensors and cameras and the watchmen there leave no lack of safety when On the off chance that the bank's security signals are sounded, 500 troopers from the base camp *will rush into the bank at the same time. In addition, the bank's security chief was previously the commander of Spain's counter-terrorism force. Now Walter's team was facing an army that would attack the bank in any situation.*

In addition, Walter's team had no knowledge of the map inside the safe, so they needed two keys and the security chief's fingerprints to get a coin into the safe. The team decides to break into the bank for

Tom and Simon Safai Karamchari, Lorraine has come to sell insurance after examining the priceless paintings and keeps the two keys in the safes behind the paintings when the security chief takes Lorraine into the room. As he was leaving, Lorraine followed him to the first painting room, Klaus hacked into the camera in the bank, then recorded Lorraine scanning the painting and played the same footage in slow motion. Lorraine opened the safe and copied the pattern of the key placed there but suddenly the bank director came there and there were only 20 seconds left before the camera was activated again. When he got to the center, Lorraine made up her mind to leave him behind to take her picture, and at that moment the director was out of the footage. According to what was supposed to be done, the real safe was just below the meeting room.

Tom Toran hid under the table and started scanning with his machine, but then suddenly some people came to have a meeting there. Now Tom has slipped under the table. After a while of fiddling,

Tom enacted the machine and the output was finished, however before that, Kalam was initiated and the security boss scoured the whole bank. Then the troopers left for the bank from the front, while Lorraine had made a copy of the subsequent key, the head of the bank came to take it, in the hood she neglected to return the first key. That Lorraine took this debris and Tom went to the third floor and he put the refuse and shut the protected, then, at that point, out of nowhere he figured out that this watchman was coming into the room. Subsequent to hearing that he was unable to hear the security signal in light of the headphones, the gatekeeper let him go lastly his central goal was achieved. The fact that there is water here makes it comprehended. Initially, the safe was based on a scale and when the heaviness of the protected changes when the safe is opened, the protected will nearby itself and simultaneously it will be loaded with water. It was understood that to get into the protected, they need to adjust the heaviness of the protected, then, at that point, Tom began attempting to keep the weight equivalent constantly, and he observed that Tom's words were valid.

It was constructed, yet it weighed 100% of the heaviness of the zero belt, and one more issue remained before them.

The walls of this underground chamber were made of titanium steel, which was solid to such an extent that it would require fifteen days to penetrate it. Walter's group has very little to finish the mission so they at last surrender. Presently Walter is disappointed and goes to the rooftop and sees that the roads are packed with football fans. At the point when he arrived, he understood that every one of the cameras would be on the group at the Verand Cup Finals, and that is the point at which his brain streaked. Indeed, we said, very much like that, they can gather the scales at the lower part of the pantry, it will take a ton of fluid nitrogen, okay, upon the arrival of the Spain versus Netherlands football match, they choose to complete their arrangement, they have job well done. With just 105 minutes to do, he originally arrived at the top of the bank by means of a zip line and bounced down through a glass hatch. Then, at that point, Klaus showed his hacking abilities and then again, the group opened the protected with the assistance of two keys and fingerprints.

Because of the response, the ground of the vault additionally began to freeze, while the group surged inside and attempted to take a similar box, yet the other and the bank's security group came to be familiar with the open window on the rooftop and they immediately opened the vault and began moving towards it. The crate fell into Lorraine's hands, yet what occurred next knocked everybody's socks off. Initially, James was a spy. As they had the option to escape from here, the impact of the fluid nitrogen on the scales beneath finished, which initiated the vault's security framework. Presently Tom, Lorraine, and James were caught in the vault and the water started to quickly rise. James was a previous officer. So swimming itcame and he took off with the crate.

Meanwhile, the chief of security called an emergency and his men with weapons were running to cure the safe. They could have drowned now they had no choice but then

Tom's brain went on and he asked Simon to add more weight to the scales so that the whole machinery seemed to be completely filled with water. *Finally, he put his radio up and the weight of the scales increased suddenly according to the system. As soon as they opened the door, they lost consciousness because there was no one in the safe. Suddenly Lorraine remembered that the director always kept his window open in the room where she had gone to scan the painting. I got lost, the warriors pursuing them and every one of the vans went off the deep end with euphoria. In such a group, the officers couldn't follow Tom and Lorraine, lastly the two of them got away. Following a couple of days, James gave the taken box to his chief. Dia and when they figure out the area of the fortune, it has the area of the Eiffel Pinnacle, then they recall that it's anything but a security area and Walter's group evaded them. The group was having some good times in a ruzot when they found the area of the genuine fortune from the container then they figured out that the fortune was concealed in the Bank of Britain after that their group prepared for another new mission.After a couple of days, James gave the taken box to his chief and when they found the fortune, it contained the area of the Eiffel Pinnacle, then, at that point, they recalled that it was anything but a security area and Walter's group.*

Toward the end, there is a summation that Tom and Legend presently Walter's group are having a good time in a stratagem that they find the area of the genuine fortune from the case when they figure out that the fortune is concealed in the Bank of Britain.

From that point forward, his group prepared for another new missionAfter a couple of days, James gave the taken box to his chief and when they found the fortune, it contained the area of the Eiffel Pinnacle, then, at that point, they recalled that it was anything but a security area and Walter's group.

Toward the end, there is a summary that Tom and Legend presently Walter's group are having a great time in a stratagem that they find the area of the genuine fortune from the container when they figure out that the fortune is concealed in the Bank of Britain. From that point onward, his group prepared for another new mission

TheEnd.

www.ingramcontent.com/pod-product-compliance
Lightning Source LLC
Chambersburg PA
CBHW071001220526
45471CB00007B/3120